CW01269956

Subtle Medicine

Subtle Medicine

Poems by
Joey Doherty

Copyright © 2021 Joey Doherty

All rights reserved

First edition

First print: November 2021

Published by Student of the Moment, LLC

Cover art by Luis Flores

Author headshot by Sydney Palmer Photo

ISBN: 979-8-9853522-0-7

A Letter to the Reader

We owe it all to the elements.

The visible and invisible threads
weaving this wild world together.

Fire. Wind. Earth. Water.

Somewhere along the way,
we've lost touch with them.
The natural world has become a distant relative,
rather than an intimate part of us.

This book is my attempt
to bring us closer to the elements.

Poem by poem.
Word by word.
Breath by breath.

The natural world misses us,
so let's reconnect.

As always, four trees will be planted
for every book sold.

Thank you for helping our planet.

- Joey

We become the *Fire*
through passion.

We become the *Wind*
through freedom.

We become the *Earth*
through grounding.

We become the *Water*
through flowing with life.

Contents

Fire

Lighting the Way

When you're unsure
if things will change in your favor,
wake up early
and watch the sunrise.

In the span of a few minutes,
you will see just how quickly
transformation can happen
from deep red
to orange
to bright yellow
when the sun focuses
on its dharma
in this life,
lighting the way
for us all.

The Fire Sings

How marvelous it must feel
to be an early flame
of a great *Fire*.

Each spark comes
from somewhere ancient,
some eternal singing flame,
never from nothing.

Bringing life
while flirting with death
and sometimes even
bringing life
through death.

It's All Love

Look up at the sky
and you will see.

Look down at your bare feet
and you will see.

Look all around
to the north
and south
and east
and west
and into the past
and present
and future
and however deep
your heart is willing to go
and you will see.

It's all Love
or simply Love
that has fallen asleep
for a time.

Mad with Meaning

I'm going mad with meaning
trying to fit seven lifetimes
into this one lovely brief life.

Too many mountains to climb.

Too many passions
to turn into half-baked careers.

Too many musicians
to listen to while lying on the floor.

Too many magical ways
to give and receive love in all forms.

Too many books with pages
I know will transform me.

Too many trees to meet
and thank for their timeless gift of air.

Too many unsent letters.

Too many unsent prayers
to no one in particular.

Too much beauty
and too little time,
or maybe it's all just enough
for one ripe go of it.

She is nurturing,
like the Great Mother of all things.

She is cheerful,
like the cosmic giggle.

She is light,
like the orange leaf blowing in the *Wind*.

She is dynamic,
like the salty sweet rocky soft ocean floor.

She is intentional,
like the *Wind* only blowing when it needs to.

She is beautiful,
like the shimmering crest of a wave crashing upwards.

She is brave,
for allowing the medicine to flow through her.

She is misunderstood,
like the holy serpent.

She is strong,
like the river gently pushing the current along.

She is potent,
like the great whale radiating deep sonic waves.

She is intelligent,
like the frog mastering both land and water.

She is sensual,

like the sunlight flirting with itself.

She is witty,
like the hummingbird swiftly coming
around the corner.

She is curious,
like the eagle swooping towards land
more often than expected.

She is worthy,
like the first ancestor to harness *Fire*.

When I Die

Place my body in a wooden canoe
like the Vikings
and light the boat on *Fire*
just before pushing me off to sea.

Let the *Fire*
reintegrate me back into the *Earth*.

Let the *Wood* of the canoe
hold me one final time
before sending me off
to become a young tree
for the next ripe body.

Let the *Water* beneath me
soon wrap all around me
and eventually become me.

Let the *Wind*
blow me deeper and deeper
into the sea
until I am no longer visible from shore,
no longer separate from you
and the *Fire*
and the *Wood*
and the *Water*
and the *Wind*.

Until I become part of it all.

Until I return Home.

Nothing Quite Like It

There is no musician quite like Love.
No painter like Love.
No poet like Love.
No photographer like Love.
No creator like Love.
No decision-maker like Love.
No speaker like Love.
No listener like Love.
No silence like Love.

There is no life
quite like one
filled with Love.

Much Too Grand

I am here to climb trees
and hike beautiful trails
and be one with Nature
and bake cookies
and dance in the kitchen while they burn
and write silly poems
and Love big
and question everything
and believe everything
and go mad with meaning
and become a new person every year
and approach the cracks in Life with grace
and seal a few of them myself
and never fully "get it"
and celebrate the fact that this existence
is much too grand to wrap my head around.

So I will wrap my soul
around it all instead.

Couldn't Hide Your Light if You Tried

"How did you find me?"

Asks the Sun
while hiding behind the curtain.

"Well you light up
everything and everyone around you,
plus you set the curtain on *Fire*
while pretending to be smaller
than you really are!"

Says the amused Moon.

Let It Be You

Know what to leave unwritten
and what to write yourself.

And when you're the one with the pen,
make sure you're writing your own story,
not the story of others
or the story you've been told to write.

Your walls will be covered in beautiful words,
words from all over the world
and all over the range of human emotion.

Let it all be you.

See yourself in the moments.

When you're crying and you look deeply within,
let it be you who is there.

When you're laughing and you look deeply within,
let it be you who is there.

When you're unsure of anything
and you look deeply within,
let the uncertainty envelope you so fully
that no matter what decision you make next,
that decision is for you.

The Great Uniter

"Who among you
is greater than Love?"

A distant voice asks.

"Is it you, anger?"

"Is it you, fear?"

"Is it you, pleasure?"

All proudly stood up
but slowly began to sit back down,
one by one kneeling before Love,
the Great Uniter
and keeper of all that is sacred,
all that lasts.

Once the Smoke Clears

When the pressure builds,
let it blow.

The volcano does not wait
a second too long
to let go
and you must not wait
another second
to allow yourself
to feel.

What comes may be *Fire*
or smoke
or lava that ends life
only to create more life.

So let it flow.

Those new and beautiful paths
come from the destruction
of your past self,
when you denied
half of your face,
but now you honor all of you,
all pieces of your *Fire*.

So let it flow.

Once the smoke clears,
you will see.

The Center of Love

What's it like
at the center of Love?

Not the outskirts,
not the shaded underbelly,
I mean the great flaming core of it all.

When it pains you
and you're going through Hell
but you're still at the center
and you go a step further
and become the center.

You become Love.

It's a Feeling

Do you trust yourself
enough
to listen
to your heart
and not
your head?

What If

What if every decision is either based in Love
or fear and you chose Love?

What if every word out of your mouth
came from Love?

What if every step you took came from Love?

What if you turned around
and Loved what you saw in a stranger's eyes?

What if every phone call you answered
or dialed was from Love?

What if every email you sent or received
was from Love?

What if everything you purchased
was based on Love?

What if everything you put in your body
was based on Love for your body?

What if everything you read online
was based on Love for your mind?

What if you viewed the detours in life
through Love's lens?

What if you looked at your mistakes with Love?

What if you channeled the bird's eye view
and saw your pain through Love?

What if every time you closed your eyes
you felt Love?

What if every seed you planted
was carefully chosen with Love?

What if you watered your plants with Love?

What if you watered your heart with Love?

What if out of all the stars in the sky
there wasn't one you didn't Love?

What if out of all the humans on this planet
there wasn't one you didn't Love?

What if out of all the thoughts in your head
there wasn't one you didn't Love?

What if it's really not that complicated
to give and receive Love?

What if it was never about wanting something
but about Loving everything?

What if throughout your heavy days
you still found something to Love?

What if you disagreed from a place of Love?

What if everything you owned you Loved?

What if you woke up and allowed
the Love deep down to come to the surface?

What if every thought about yourself
or another was from Love?

What if your boundaries were set with Love?

What if you looked at the sky and saw Love?

What if you looked down at your feet
and felt Love?

What if you Loved the moon
as much as the moon Loves you?

What if you Loved the Universe
as much as the Universe Loves you?

What if you gave up everything
that wasn't
big
pure
unadulterated Love?

The Nectar of Connection

There is no attachment
between the flower and the bee.

They nourish each other
and then go their separate ways.

Maybe meeting again,
maybe not.

And either outcome is fine.

The important thing
is that their connection
changed them both.

Forever.

For the better.

Like a Child

Let's visit a park
and lie down on the grass
and turn off our phones
and watch the clouds
all afternoon
without saying a word,
except for:

"Wow!"
"Did you see that one?!"
"What does it look like to you?"
"I see a unicorn."
"I feel like a child."
"Life is magic."

They Are a Gift

Friends who know you.
Who really get you.

Friends who bring out your best.
Your authenticity. Your light.

Friends who challenge you.

Friends who remind you how far you've come.

Friends who know how to sit with you.
Be with you. Really listen.

Friends who feel like home.

Friends who ask the big questions, like:

"How is your heart today?"
"What's our next adventure?"
"Will this decision bring you closer to your dreams?"
"Where is the magic in your life?"
"Where is there room for more?"

Primal Mirrors

If I am a reflection of you
and you are a reflection of me
and everything visible
and invisible to us
is carefully bound together
like the very first primal drum
that beats to all the hearts
of the Universe,
why not turn up the volume
by living as fully as possible,
making a big shiny dance
of it all.

Joey Doherty

You Are Magic

Who told you that magic
and passion
had to be unstable?

When was this lie born?

There's magic inside all of us,
but some wear it more proudly
and are more acquainted
with this realm
than others.

They flirt with insanity
a little more often.

But magic does not equal insane.

And I'm not talking about
the kind of magic on television
where a rabbit is pulled out of a hat.

I'm talking about
the kind of magic
where you pull life
out of yourself.

They ask,

"How do we live
both for the moment
and for future generations?"

She smiles,

"They are one in the same
when the moment is built on Love,
not fear."

Say It Often

I deserve healthy Love. I deserve passionate and magical and balanced Love. I deserve for my voice and boundaries to be heard and honored. I deserve to be seen as the kind person I am, not tricked into thinking I am less. I deserve someone who has the capacity to love me in a true way. I deserve someone who knows how to disagree without sounding the alarms and unleashing the wolves and destroying the peace of a whole neighborhood. I deserve to feel safe. With my words. My steps. My sensitivity so that I know my big heart won't be weaponized. I deserve to know where we stand. I deserve to have trust flow back and forth between us like a never-ending gust of *Wind* passing from my mouth when I speak to her ears as she listens and so it goes back and forth and back and forth, even when the breeze softens and especially when the hurricanes arrive. I deserve to be seen. I deserve to never be manipulated and always treated with respect. I deserve everything that I am willing and able to give, and it is finally time to accept nothing less.

What Are You Craving?

"What is the meaning of it all?"
They ask.

"To be fully here,"
She says.

To fully taste life as it comes.
To pull Love closer rather than push it away.
To sink into the moments.
To trust it all.
To crave a mango and then eat that mango.
To crave a drive and then take that drive.

To crave Love
and then create
that boundless Love.

Do You Remember?

Your purpose.
Your godliness.
Your power.
Your softness.
Your ancestors.
Your magic.

Your name.
The one beneath the surface,
beneath the words.

Your ability to trust. In the world.
In your neighbor. In yourself.

Your place here. On this planet. In this moment.

Your lovely ability to feel alive.

Your touch and your gaze.
Healing through the senses.

Your uncontrollable desire to Love.
Even when it's scary.

Your breath.
In sync with that internal flowing wave.

Your ability to be amazed.
Your inner child.

Excited over something small

that's actually something rather big.

Your power to define
what your life looks and feels like.

Your never-ending cravings for more.
More balance.
More Love.
More life.

From Dark to Light

Anyone close
to the light
has once
intimately known
the dark.

Thinker or Feeler

"I'm a good thinker."

Says the proud Sun.

"Lovely,
and how are you at feeling?"

Asks the smirking Moon.

Drawing Board

If your goal is to be famous,
go back to the drawing board.

You've missed it.

If your goal is to be quoted
by people all over the world,
go back to the drawing board.

You've missed it.

If your goal is to be enlightened
for any reason at all,
go back to the drawing board.

You've missed it.

What's the drawing board,
you ask?

It's Life,
my friend.

Pure, fiery, never quite
big or small enough,
Life.

Heart Opener

I want to be a heart-opener.

Cacao in human form.

Can opener of Love
gently prying open your heart
and stuffing a little more
of yourself
inside that living
breathing
beating
Life.

Do They Know Your Heart?

Tell me,
how many letters
have you written
in your mind
and never sent?

Love is Now

The present moment is Love
and Love is the present moment.

Love comes from everywhere
and extends everywhere.

Love is timeless,
boundless,
less of a feeling
and more of a being.

And I'm not only talking
about romantic Love.

I'm talking about Love
as a way of life,
spanning generations
and emanating
from that eternal here and now
inside each of us,
within reach
at any given moment.

That Can Be Heaven

"Are you in Love?" She asks.

I laugh, "Yes, aren't you?!"

I'm in Love with it all.
This whole world.
This whole existence.
This marvelous roller coaster of a life,
and I don't even like roller coasters!

But that doesn't matter, you see,
because once you've tasted
the bliss and the unity
in all the mundane and maddening moments,
everything is heaven.

The detours you don't plan,
because we never do plan them,
they can be heaven.

The ordinary left and right,
to and fro, that can be heaven.

The relationships ending,
that's heaven, somewhere in there.

The days that just don't go your way,
heaven.

All of it,
heaven.

Wind

Soar On

To us, life seems to be full of unlimited choices.

To the Universe,
we're all just a brief flap
of the butterfly's wings
and there's only one way it could all go.

One beautiful direction to fly.

So loosen your grip on the details
and the decisions
and the illusion of control.

Every moment unfolds in the direction
that brings the most growth.

The butterfly couldn't soar
or land
or dance around with the *Wind*
quite as gracefully
if every flap of his wings
was carefully calculated with the mind.

He knows better than to weigh down
his short innocent life
with too much seriousness.

"Live lightly," he says.

"Forget about control and soar on,
moment by moment."

Have You Ever Felt That?

Have you ever felt the *Wind* move through you?
Not around you, not weaving around your body,
your head, your legs, not acting as if you're a wall or
a door it needs to move around, but instead you act
as an open, completely open vessel for the *Wind* to
surge through, passing right through you, in and out.
No clinging involved. Incredibly seamless, so that it's
no longer Nature and you, it's simply Nature, which
includes you. And you and the *Wind* are dancing.

Have you ever felt that?

Where the *Wind* feels like home. And you feel like
home to the *Wind*. It's a sacred reciprocity. "Hello
again," you both say to each other, without words.
Just presence. Just each other's pure essence. The
most valuable form of currency there is.

Have you ever felt that?

Where the *Wind* is so familiar to you and you are so
familiar to it that it's friends meeting again, a
friendship that goes back and back and back in time.
An ancient relationship. The same *Wind* your
ancestors breathed in and out.

Have you ever felt that, deep in your bones?
Have you remembered?

When the *Wind* is more than the name we have

given it. You know it's much more than we can comprehend with our limited human words. You allow the *Wind* to be much more elusive, mysterious, deep than you are capable of knowing with your human intellect. But you are capable, you know, of feeling it. Of being with the *Wind*. Of living the moment so fully that the *Wind* feels seen by you. Have you ever felt that? The *Wind* feeling seen by you. Nature feeling seen by you, which is really just Nature seeing Nature. The birds too, the birds feeling seen by you. The trees too, the insects, the stars, the moon, the tall grass dancing in an open field with the *Wind,* all while you are also dancing with it all, as you move through life and follow the natural course of things. None of it can be fully described. It can't be explained. You can't do it with words. You can only do it with being.

So tell me,
have you ever felt that?

As Freely as the Breath

Just as natural as it is
to open your eyes
and take that first conscious breath
of the day,
so too it is to Love.

Giving Love.
Receiving Love.
Being Love.

So how will you remember?

How will you allow Love
to move through you
as freely as the breath travels
from your lungs
to the *Wind*
to the world
and finally back to yourself
to begin again?

How will you clear the way?

What are you waiting for?

Why Not Laugh?

Let's get existential
in a playful way.

Let's talk about why we're here
and where we come from
and where we're going
and laugh
with relief
because there are no answers
quite grand enough
to satisfy
these big
beautiful
unquenchable
questions.

Open Roads

I drove across the country
to show myself something new.

To remind myself that it's all a miracle.

To jog my memory of all that is sacred.

To wake back out of reality.

To sink back into the depth of my being.

To meet eyes with more strangers.

To cling to no person or mountain or tree,
while deeply admiring them all.

To remember the beauty.
To see the beauty.
To be the beauty,
once again.

Where to Next?

What you once knew
is changing.

The road is long
and winding
and beautiful.

At times you'll feel up in the clouds
and others you'll feel somewhere else.

Comfort has been flipped on its head,
for a time.

The day has come
to trust the seasons within seasons
and the Gods within your godliness
and the time outside of time's societal embrace.

Keep re-writing your story.

Not even the lines on the map
are carved in stone.

One Day

One day,
I'll no longer desire
the safety of guidelines
and boxes
and shoes on my feet.

One day,
I'll begin dancing
to every song
that comes through my speakers.

One day,
I'll wake up to Love
in all forms
and all moments.

One day,
I'll become free.

One day,
I'll become myself.

And I can see now,
that day
I've been waiting for,
is today.

I Bet You Can

Can you dance
through the uncertainty?

Can you allow Life
to move through you?

Can you let a sunrise
be a sunrise
and a sunset
be a sunset?

Can you surrender?

Unearthing Your Wild Side

It's all about removing your blocks
and unlearning
the self-imposed rules
holding you back.

We can all dance.

Will you remove the blocks
keeping you from dancing
without reservation?

We can all sing.

Will you remove the blocks
keeping your from singing
without reservation?

We can all Love.

Will you remove the blocks
keeping you from Loving
without reservation?

It's simple.
It's freedom.
It's unearthing your wild side.

The Art of Release

I am practicing the art
of releasing anything
that no longer serves me.

Old beliefs.
Old clothes.
Old ways of living.

Releasing something good
to allow for something better.

Give it to the birds.
They know what to do.

Let the feather fall
when it needs to
and look down
with gratitude.

Over Here

Be yourself
so undeniably
that the Universe
knows exactly
where to send
the magic.

Softer This Way

She dries her clothes outside
in the fresh air
wearing that flowy skirt
and favorite thrift store tee
with the sunflower over the heart
and all those holy whites
and browns
and natural fabrics
that came directly from the *Earth*
and she says
they are softer this way,
the clothes,
because the *Wind* is allowed to play
with the cotton seed it planted long ago
and the silkworm is allowed to see
its masterpiece flowing with grandfather *Wind*
and the sun is allowed to lighten the colors
because that's what the sun does best
and she says
it's almost as if the *Earth* is kissing her clothes
with all the secrets of the animal kingdom
and all the mysteries found deep in the forest
and all the lovely unseen pieces
of the natural world
that often go unnoticed
except by her
and the rest of us
who still know the language
of our great ancient flowing Mother
we call home.

The Big Questions

How we got here.
Why we're here.
Where we're going after we die.

I have no clue what I believe
and I Love that,
with a big smile on my face.

Because these questions
are much too expansive
to be dulled with human answers.

The moment we try to name it,
we miss it.

So I don't name it anymore.

I just live it.
I just feel it.
I just trust it.

And that is plenty for me.

Anything Could Happen

I like a blank canvas.

An empty page.

A new day
with the sunlight
peeking through
my east-facing windows.

Are You Dancing?

Life becomes simple
when you know what you want
and almost ritualistically
look that thing in the eye.

Staring deeply into its soul
until you remember
that your essence is in there.

It has been all along!

Now we're getting somewhere,
you think.

Now it's all starting to make sense.

Until eventually you lose focus again,
only to circle back to yourself
once more
and on and on and on it goes.

None of this is easy,
but it doesn't have to be complicated.

It doesn't have to be chaos.
It can be a beautiful dance.

So tell me,
are you dancing?

Bliss Without a "Because"

Once you've tasted it,
people will get suspicious,
concerned,
deeply and unconsciously jealous.

Don't mind them.

That's their work,
not yours.

Keep riding the directionless bliss
and see where it takes you.

We're All Artists

It is not, "Are you an artist?"

It is, "What is your art?"

Do you paint the *Earth* with your bare feet?

Are your taste buds the canvas?

Does your voice play with the *Wind*?

How do your thoughts paint your reality?

Is your art in the past, present, or future?

What grand stories are found in your dreams?

How does your first memory
create a tapestry with your latest memory?

Do you whistle or hum or sing
when you're overjoyed?

A Tough Lesson

Feeling fully seen
and fully understand
is ultimately
an inside job.

Intention and Release

It's a subtle dance,
floating somewhere
between intention and release.

Technique and letting go.

The push of the *Wind*
with the pull of the rapids.

How and Why

A man who spends his days
acquiring great success
and money
and fame
has lived far less
than a man
who spends his days
silently sitting in a field
listening to the *Wind*
play with the tall grass.

It's not about what
you spend your time doing,
it's how
and why.

Golden and Free

Tossing seeds into the *Wind*
at sunset
with a slightly open hand
and a wide open heart
wearing that thrift store dress
she feels most free in,
hopeful for whatever comes
in-between Now
and the flower-filled Now
of tomorrow.

Joey Doherty

What Else is There?

He fell in Love
with the process.

Countless Ways to Be

Don't take any of it too seriously.

Chase the floating leaf
for a mile downstream
or sit and patiently watch it sail by
or even be the one
who impatiently
throws it in the river upstream,
turning it into a reckless sailboat.

It doesn't matter,
just be here
and enjoy the hell out of this life.

Joey Doherty

There Are No Rules

Roll the windows down
while driving in the rain.

Walk around barefoot.

Talk to trees.

Use that vacation time
to work on your dream project.

Dance without music through the streets.

Love big without expectations.

Be yourself, undeniably.

Here I Am

He sat down
and remembered who he was.

He climbed the tree
and remembered who he was.

He grew out his hair
and remembered who he was.

He trusted the flow of things
and remembered who he was.

There was no one left to be,
but himself.

Flowing Freely

When you unblock yourself.
When you no longer let yourself remain stagnant.
When you allow the energy to flow through you.

You not only open up the airways
for your own energy
but you open up the Universe too,
because you are the Universe,
you are Nature,
there is no separation.

So as you unblock yourself,
as you no longer let yourself remain stagnant,
as you open up your energetic airways,
you are also opening up the Universe's airways.

And so things flow,
for you,
for all.

Life becomes you.
You become Life.

If You Want to Know Me

If you want to know me,
look to the moon.

If you want to know me,
watch the *Wind* play with the leaves.

If you want to know me,
my words are not the key.

If you want to know me,
know yourself.

If you want to know me,
know that you are God
and I am God
and it's all holy holy holy
and then forget this knowing
and finally sink into a deep feeling
and eventually
once you join the eternal Now
you will see,
it was never about knowing me
or knowing yourself,
but simply about
being being being
and living in this free state,
the truest form of expression
we have.

Joey Doherty

The Answers are Within

We try to force inspiration.

We scroll and scroll and read and read,
frantically searching for a quick and easy quote
that will give us all the answers, connect the dots,
bring us closer to some idolized form
of enlightenment that's no longer serving the world
but solely serving ourselves.

You won't find the answer in another's quote.
You won't find the answer in my poems.

The secrets of your Universe
are not found in another's Universe.

It's in the moments, your moments.

The conversations and adventures and deep thoughts
while walking from the living room to the kitchen.

It's in the most mundane
and also the most extraordinary of situations.

So don't pass off your healing
and your meaning to another.

Let's learn from each other,
but let's keep both lanes open.

Learning and teaching, teaching and learning,
from lifetime to lifetime to lifetime.

Let's Come Back

I wake up as myself
and fall asleep as myself,
but something happens
in-between
during those automatic hours
when I am more of a cog in the machine
than the machine itself,
more of a mind
than a soul,
more of who they want me to be
than who I truly am.

Sacred Directions

We are all walking around a little lost
and in a childlike way
seeking directions from each other.

We ask,
"Where is God?
Where can I find Love?
When did you last see them?"

So people give us
the best directions they can
based on their own world.

They say,
"I took the second unassuming left
next to the Big Tree
and then honestly
I don't know what happened
but a giant boulder fell from the cliff
and forced me to go another way,
which is exactly where I needed to go,
where I found what I was looking for."

So my advice?
Listen to the boulders.
Your boulders.
Allow for detours.

Maybe that's exactly where the meaning lies.

Sometimes
the eagle
walks
and sometimes
the human
soars.

Joey Doherty

How Many Hours Would You Need?

To change the world.
To write the book.
To cultivate peace.
To notice the little things.
To become yourself.

Why Cling?

I don't like to be too strict
with any of my beliefs
or ways of life.

It's all constantly changing
and that includes myself,
so why cling?

Of course,
there's the universal truth
underneath it all,
which is Love.

Being Love
and giving Love
and feeling Love.

But apart from that,
anything above Love's surface
is simply a different shade of its essence.

Different words
and Gods
and approaches for the same thing.

So I hold close what I know to be true,
that we are all woven together
with Love and Beauty
as our thread and needle
and I allow the rest to come and go
with the seasons.

Dancing with Bliss

"Is bliss still dancing around
with you this morning?"

She asks.

"Yes, we've become
quite good dance partners,"
I say,

"Once I decided to cherish
her unpredictability
rather than fear it,
allow her to lead
rather than attempt
to direct every move,
we became the best of dance partners."

Earth

Plant, Tend, Harvest

When feeling stuck,
ask yourself:

Is this a time
to plant,
to tend,
or to harvest?

Sacred Reciprocity

You're seen by Nature,
but does Nature feel seen by you?

You're heard by Nature,
but does Nature feel heard by you?

You're honored by Nature,
but does Nature feel honored by you?

You're Loved by Nature,
but does Nature feel Loved by you?

Everywhere I Look

I sifted through the spider webs
and the branches
and the sunlight flirting with the leaves
and what I found
was God everywhere I looked,
Love everywhere I looked,
myself everywhere I looked.

Keeping the Beat

With all the sounds of the *Earth*.
With all the *Winds* of time.

Let it be clear
that this life is alive.

This life is ours.

Those present
and those passed
and those to come.

Those who walk
and those who soar.

We all live
within the great beating heart
of it all
and we are also
the ones
keeping the beat steady.

Unspoken Language

Trusting your intuition
isn't simply trusting yourself.

It's trusting every ancestor
who paved the way
and passed on this deep knowing
we all have in our bones
that's meant to grow stronger
with each generation.

Every time you listen
and trust
and honor this knowing,
you are continuing
this unspoken language
and power
that no one can take away.

You may not always like
where your intuition
is guiding you in the moment,
but that's what it's all about.

Trust.
Trust
A little more trust.

Pruning

There's only so much room
in a garden
and only so much room
in a life.

Do you like
what you're filling yours with?

Is the dream
allowed to sprout?

What is Your Deep Knowing?

The thing you knew
the moment
you were brought into this world.

The thing you will take with you
to the next.

The thing that comes natural.

The thing that lights you up.

The thing you feel
deep
deep
in your bones.

Which Role Suits You Best?

We take turns
playing seed
and flower.

Playing God
and human.

Playing the creator
and the created.

Pure Truth

There is a truth
to the natural world.

Words
and buildings
and long stretches of sterile time
always fall short.

But Nature.

Wildly beautiful
and brutal Nature.

That's pure truth,
always.

Soften

The tough roots
survive the storm,
but it's the soft roots
that grow through it,
allowing the heavy rain
to move and shape
their days to come.

Just Us

This morning
I quietly watched a robin
search for a worm in my front yard
with the cars rushing by
and the construction workers
with their clanging metal music
and the sun finally coming out
after a big rain
and somehow
it was still just the bird and me,
a big trust and connection
between species
within the madness of a city.

Low Sun, High Moon

One summer day,
I harvested a flower at peak sunset
and dried those petals
under a full moon
and every sip
of that otherworldly tea
brought me closer
to finally understanding
the secrets whispered
under sun's fiery breath
and finally hearing the songs sung
under moon's quiet watch.

Simply Being

I found myself craving the light,
running from the dark.

But there is no light
without dark.

There is little choice
when it comes to a moment.

Actually, there is no choice at all.

You're simply there
in that specific location,
with that specific person,
with a specific sequence of events
to get you where you are,
and you enjoy.

You soak it up.
There is no choice.
There is simply being.

It's Called Living

I'm sitting here
daydreaming
about this moment.

Wait a minute!

Worlds Within You

When you have both worlds within you,
it can feel overwhelming.

Spirit and worldy.
Light and dark.
Up and down.
East and West.

A lot for one person
to be tapped into.

So rest easy.

Dull the noise if you need to,
but not forever.

You are meant
to fully experience
all the worlds within you.

Can You See?

It's all sacred
when you know
how to look.

Here Comes Growth

The bigger the storm,
the deeper the tree's roots
once the rain blows over.

This is when growth
bursts forth
from within.

Be patient
and you will see.

Living as Meditation

While walking,
intentionally walk.

While breathing,
intentionally breathe.

While drinking your morning cacao,
intentionally drink.

While listening to music,
intentionally listen.

While eating,
intentionally eat.

While scrolling social media,
intentionally scroll.

While reading that book,
intentionally read.

While listening to a friend talk,
intentionally listen.

While living this life,
intentionally live.

Joey Doherty

Co-Authors

Your story
and the planet's story
are not
separate.

Full Moon Ceremony

No hiding tonight.

The beauty in Nature
is simply a reflection of our own beauty,
she says.

We can only know Nature
as intimately as we know ourselves,
and we can only know ourselves
as intimately as we know Nature.

She is us.
We are Her.

So drop the act.
Tune in.

Get lost wandering around your soul.

Inhale part of your ancestors
and exhale all of you.

Loosen your grip on your heart.

Give it freely.

Authentic Seasons

If *Earth* turned Her shapeless green eyes
toward you and told you
She's decided
to only foster Her relationship
with Summer from now on,
because the cold is just too much work
for Her old roots,
you would think She's lost it.

"We need Winter!
You can't just pick and choose!
What about the penguins
and glaciers
and children
who want to play in the snow?!"

We would immediately see
that *Earth* is not thinking straight.

Yet we do this all the time.
We want joy, but not sadness.
We want peace, but not anxiety.

But it's all part of the human experience
and we need the struggle
just as much as we need
the Winters.

Direct Line to God

There are certain things
that provide a direct line
to God.

They have an extra dose of holy.

What I'm talking about is
Nature,
Art,
Music,
Love,
The Moment.

Have you met them lately?

Tell Me

Do the birds know your name?

Do the trees dream of you at night?

Does the *Wind* recognize your breath?

Does the world know your heart?

From the Inside

Grow yourself
from the inside out
and those branches
of yours
and those leaves
of yours
and those deeply rooted values
of yours
will reach further
into others
than you could possibly
imagine.

Expectations

Don't expect to receive respect
from those who have little respect
for themselves.

Don't expect kindness
from those who struggle
to be kind to themselves.

Don't expect stability
from those who are not internally stable.

Don't expect a balanced love
from those who can't seem to foster this balance
in their other relationships.

Don't expect closure
when the two stories are radically different.

Don't expect to feel good around someone
who continually leaves you
feeling hardened and closed off.

Don't expect someone
to speak positively about you
when they speak negatively about others.

Don't expect someone to change
simply because you want them to change.

Letting Go

What needs
to wilt
for the dream
to sprout?

All I Have is Now

Living in the moment. Living in the unadulterated Now, is like reading a book. The most profound book you've ever read. Reading it for the first time. Without a pen. Without a highlighter. And each time you move on to the next word, that word you had just read disappears. Fades away. There's no going back. And if you try to jump ahead and predict what might happen next in the story, the page you jumped from disappears. The word you jumped from disappears. And you've lost it. You've allowed it to slip through your fingers. And there's no beating the system. You can't hover over a particularly pleasant and light word for longer than the moment allows. You can't cling to a particularly pleasant part of the story for longer than the moment allows. Or else you'll lose it So living with this eternal Now is knowing all of this and flowing with it. Allowing the story to unfold as it is. And being at peace with the impermanence of it all.

Bridges Between Worlds

There's a bridge,
multiple bridges really,
linking this world to others.

Physical to Spirit.
Reality to more reality.
Light to slightly more light.
Mundane to sacred.

What bridges do you walk?

What bridges take you
directly to a seat at the table
with the Gods within you?

What is your direct line to Source?

Mine is Nature.
Love.
Music.
Poetry.
Soul-to-Soul Connections.

Fabric of Humanity

Even if you left to be alone in the woods
for months
or years
or the remainder of this lifetime,
humanity would still
be etched into your bones.

Your ancestors still guiding you.

Every word spoken or unspoken
still part of your story.

We need each other,
and this is not something to run from.

This is something to celebrate.
To turn into a big dance.

The fabric of humanity
flows through your veins,
so you might as well flow with it
and direct the red current
toward never-ending destinations that heal,
that bring clarity,
that transform dams
into welcoming passages.

Maybe this is the purpose.

All of It

I think God
is in everything beautiful.

And everything here
is beautiful.

Water

.

There's No Turning Back Now

Once you've seen the light,
felt the natural flowing pace of Life,
turned inward enough
to remember who you are,
it's all groovy ups and downs
from here on out.

The whole play of Life
echoing across the ocean floor
and you realize
that the rest of Nature is dancing,
so why aren't we?

Keep coming back into yourself,
like a river reaching the ocean
and remembering that she too is salty,
that she too is the big sea
and the fresh stream
and even the lukewarm *Water*
inside the wide-awake human
swimming through her cold salty arms
with nothing but the body you were born into.

It can be serious.
It can also be play.
It can be whatever you'd like.

The dance is in the moments,
not the details.

While I wait for the Water to boil,
I stretch my body,
prepare it for the day,
prepare it to remain flexible
for whatever comes.

While I wait for the Water to boil,
my mind is still half-asleep
but my soul is more awake than ever,
fueled by the sun peeking over the horizon
and promises of nothing
but the sweet sweet vision of a new day.

While I wait for the Water to boil,
I can't help but wonder
how I arrived at this moment
in this tiny kitchen
with these 1970s worn tiles
and the unshakeable feeling
that this life is playing out
exactly the way it's meant to,
how I never could have imagined it would.

While I wait for the Water to boil,
something comes over me,
I feel a rush of words
but not the typical replays
and rewinds
and sentences
that have been thought before,
no these are new,
these are something to note,
something to write down
or at the very least

say out loud to no one.

While I wait for the Water to boil,
I find it so enchanting
that outside my window
the *Water* is frozen in flakes
falling from the sky
and inside my tea kettle
the *Water* is nearly bubbling
and within my own body
the *Water* is somewhere in-between,
between the freezing and the bubbling,
between two worlds.

While I wait for the Water to boil,
I get so lost in the childlike energy
of an early morning,
lost in the smoke
of the braided sweetgrass,
lost in the endless possibilities
of a new day.

Ripple Effect

Every time someone wakes up to their worth
and flips that switch
where it is no longer acceptable
to work any job
or be with any person
or live any place
that doesn't touch their soul, we all win.

No longer accepting anything less than soul.
Lighting their soul on *Fire*.
Each time someone flips that switch,
they're not only here and now,
bringing their full self,
tapping into that potential more and more,
but they encourage others to do the same.

It is the ripple effect.
It is the butterfly effect.
It is the Universe itself continually expanding
second and after second
as we go throughout history
within a single person.

And they expand and reach another star
and they expand and reach another galaxy
and they expand and reach another Universe
and they expand and everything within them
is becoming more and more true.

And free.
And beautiful.

Joey Doherty

Quenched and Mysterious

After it rains
when everything is quenched,
the forest is quiet.

Even a small acorn dropping
or *Water* droplets rolling off a leaf
or a few birds singing to each other
way off in the distance
becomes such a grand experience.

A symphony, really.

I wonder how many silent birds are here.

How many insects.

How many different mosses
and trees
and wildly unique shades of green.

Endless.
Endless.
Endless.

There's no end to Nature.
Always a bit of a mystery.
And I like the mysterious.

It's All Holy

The sky is holy.
The grass is holy.
The birds are holy.
The sun and moon are holy.
Your breath is holy.
Your joy is holy.
Your pain is holy.
Your flaws are holy.

You you you,
my friend,
are holy.

Joey Doherty

Intimate with Now

I'm not interested
in what happened yesterday
or what might happen tomorrow
or who said what to whom.

I'll sit in my backyard
drinking warm tea
and watch the squirrels
chase each other
up and down the trees.

I'll read one page of Alan Watts
and then get distracted
by the beauty right in front of me,
which is what Alan would have wanted.

I'll become so still
a bird mistakes me for a tree
and lands right on my head.

I'll get so intimate
with the eternal Now
that I laugh
as the bird poops
in my hair.

Fully Alive

We are all born into this world
fully alive.

Fully tapped into Source.

So tell me, how alive are you in this moment?

Does your breath sing of peace?

Do your movements
reflect the beauty of the world?

Do your words
echo across the ocean floor
with gentle flowing power,
singing of a Love
that transcends the physical and mental?

Tell me, how alive are you in this moment?

I'd like to see you alive.

More each day.

Primal Moments

I like moments
that don't take much thinking.

Only feeling.

Blurry photos
from untamed awe.

Primal poems
from somewhere out in the ethers.

Human connections
that foster being rather than doing.

A guitar riff
that seeps into my bones.

A surrendering to the current,
letting the rapids guide the way.

Ask Often

Dear Universe,
how is your heart today?

What can I do to help?

How can I better Love you
moving forward?

Coming Home

You can come Home
without hopping on a plane
or meeting a soulmate
or having a perfect day.

Coming Home happens within,
multiple times a day
when the Soul and Self join hands,
coming together once again
and recognizing
that the struggle can feel beautiful
and the peace can feel unusual
and it's all exactly
how it's meant to be,
when we remember
that we're already Home.

Any of It is Fine

You can climb a cliff
or you can sit at a desk
or you can drive across the country
with no real destination in mind.

Any of it is fine.

Just be all there.

Soak up the moments
like a sponge
that never runs dry.

Joey Doherty

No Separation

We have created limiting words
in an effort to understand
the most beautiful and mysterious and expansive
parts of existence,
separating them from each other
and from us.

What I'm talking about is Love,
God,
Nature,
the Moment.

We have separated them,
yet they are all the same.

And we don't have them,
we are them.

It's not Nature and us.
It's simply Nature, and we are Nature.

It's not Love and us.
It's simply Love, and we are Love.

It's not God and us.
It's simply God, and we are God too.

It's not the present moment and us.
It's simply the moment
with no real separation between us
and that eternal living breathing Now.

Ever Changing Recipe

There's no golden recipe for it all.
Life. Happiness. Freedom.

I could tell you mine,
but the moment I finish the sentence
it will have changed.

You are not me and I am not even me
after the moment has passed.

It's new
it's new
it's all new
and changing every second.

There's no predicting, so why try?
What a relief!

I'd rather ride the wave as it comes.

Go this way, go that way,
dive underneath for a while
with the coral and sharks
and wildly intricate beings
that have yet to be labeled.

Too much labeling for my taste.

We need more being and less capturing.
More living and less predicting.
More Love and less fear.

Joey Doherty

It's In the Moments

You won't find
what you're looking for
in the pages of a book
or the wisdom
of another.

Seeing and Being Seen

It's not your job
to be fully seen by others.

It is your job
to fully see them
and in doing so
you allow yourself
to be seen too.

After all,
all of it,
you looking at them
and them looking at you
is all just the Universe
looking back at itself
in subtle admiration.

Home

Home is
where the river flows.

Home is
where the heart knows.

Home is
what you consciously chose.

Becoming All

"What's the difference
between the heart and the soul?"

She asks.

The heart is *Earth*-bound
and limited in time,
brought more alive
by the beautiful matters of existence.

The soul is not bound by anything
we can accurately name,
brought more alive
by matters that transcend this plane
and will continue doing so
until it is decided by All
that it is time for a soul to rest,
and on and on and on
the Big process unfolds
now and before and always
circling round and round we go,
playfully and rhythmically
dancing with Life along the way
until eventually there is no space between,
no time separating Life's moments
from yours,
and this is when two dance partners
become All.

See For Yourself

There is so much abundance
all around us
and within us.

You can slow down time
to appreciate it all
if you choose.

With your breath,
your eyes,
your unclenched jaw,
your moments
that have nowhere to go
but within.

I Like When

I like when people use words
like "smitten"
and "adore"
and "let's make a day of it."

I like when people smile with their eyes.

I like when people turn around
because they can feel you
admiring their energy.

I like when people enjoy the rain
when it rains
and enjoy the sun
when it's sunny
and enjoy the clouds
when there's no blue to be found
up there in the sky.

I like when people are real.
They're not afraid to be real.
They see no point in putting on a mask.

I especially like when I am the one
living out these qualities
that I admire in others.

Joey Doherty

Loosen Your Grip

What happens when we let go of control?

When we loosen our grip on life?

When we accept
that there will be bumps in the road?

When we turn around
and are no longer surprised
to see pieces of ourselves
everywhere we look?

What More Could We Need?

"It's all unfolding quite nicely,
wouldn't you say?"

I say to the thawed river.

"Oh yes,
how could it not?

Breath is still in your lungs,
our Mother is still spinning
round and round,
and there are still humans
who know how to speak with me.

What more could we need?"

She says
in that universal,
flowing language.

Never and Forever

It doesn't begin or end with us.

We are a drop of *Water* in the ocean.

We are a leaf on the tree.

We are a spark of the wildfire.

We are a slowly dying insect
on Life's web
and also the spider
and the web itself.

We are human
and we are inhuman,
somehow never and forever
at the same time.

They Know a Few Secrets

Have you ever met someone,
looked into their eyes,
listened to them speak,
watched them move,
and you can sense
that this person knows things?

They know a few secrets.

They've seen the underbelly of life
and have come up for air
again and again and again
to reveal what they know
to others
simply by the way
they live their life.

Staring Back at Itself

We would be better off
if we took time
to stare into our eyes
in the mirror
and for a brief second
feel the Universe
staring back at Itself.

To get out of the city
and look up at the night sky
and for a brief second
feel the ancient stars
staring back at us.

To slow down long enough
and get lost
in the mysterious beautiful corners
of existence.

To remember who we are
and where we come from,
even for a brief second.

First, We Go Inward

Open the door
and let the sunlight in.

You need
to go inward
before you go
out.

"How can I better Love you?"

Asks the Clouds.

"Open the sky
when I'm feeling bright
and cover me up
when I'm feeling dark."

Says the Sun.

Call Yourself Home

Call yourself home
at least once a day.

Call yourself home
and remember to play.

Call yourself home
in the morning
and night.

Call yourself home,
it'll be alright.

Joey Doherty

Waves of Now

In a crowded sea
of tomorrows,
be today.

The Whole Sobbing Way

I'll take my time
with this whole enlightenment business
because I'd like at least another 3,000 lifetimes
just to listen to all the music
and another 2,000 to hug all the people
who didn't get enough Love
and another couple thousand
to smell enough flowers
to help humans evolve
toward the ability to smell deep truth
and once I can taste that sweet sweet
Buddha bliss around the corner
I'll take one final lifetime
to wipe my mind clean
of all the secrets of the Universe
and realize that the very essence
of what it means to be human,
the very unconscious essence we all have
from the moment we come into existence
is no different than the conscious realization
we have upon enlightenment.

We come into this world crying
but not knowing why
and we realize our way out of this world
still crying
but doing so with the knowing
that all the rivers and oceans and drops
of crashing thunder rain
are behind you and truly are you
the whole beautiful sobbing way.

There You Are

Beneath the cars rushing by
and the air conditioners running
and the pitter patter
of everyday life speeding by,
there are the birds,
the trees,
the *Wind*,
the subtle
yet magnificent dark sky.

Beneath the noise,
there is stillness.

Beneath the thoughts,
there
you
are.

Subtle Medicine

Thank You

I am endlessly grateful
for those who are keeping
the language of the elements
alive and well.

To my ancestors,
for passing on this deep wisdom
that I'm starting to unearth
more and more each day.

To you,
for wanting to immerse yourself
more deeply into the Earth's teachings.

If you ask me,
as long as poetry
is still written and read,
we'll be alright
on this wild
and spinning
and very much alive rock
we get to call home.

About the Author

Joey Doherty is a licensed professional counselor, podcast host, and founder of Creatives Gone Hiking. He often lectures on creativity, spirituality, self-love, nature therapy, compassion fatigue, and meditation. He enjoys rock climbing, slack lining, barefoot hiking, and playing drums. Joey currently lives in Columbus, Ohio.

Instagram
@joeydoherty

Email
joeygdoherty@gmail.com

Website
www.joeydoherty.com

Other Books by Joey Doherty

Student of the Moment (2020)
Color the World (2019)
Wild Compass (2018)
Remember to Harvest (2017)

If you enjoyed this book and feel called
to write a review on Amazon or Good Reads,
it would mean the world to me.

- Joey

Printed in Great Britain
by Amazon

77648822R00099